VIA FOLIOS 84

Mystics in the Family

Poems by
MARIA FAMÀ

BORDIGHERA PRESS

Grateful acknowledgment is made to the editors of the following publications where some of these poems first appeared:

Avanti Popolo; *Breaking Open*; *Descant*; *Liberty Hill Poetry Review*; *Paterson Literary Review*; *Philadelphia Poets*; *The Poet*; *Schuylkill Valley Journal*; and *Sweet Lemons*

"The Infant of Prague with a Black Eye" was awarded an Editor's Choice Award in the 2008 Allen Ginsberg Poetry Awards.

"My Mother's Prayer List" was awarded the 2006 Amy Tritsch Needle Award for Poetry.

Library of Congress Control Number: 2012952641

©2013 by Maria Famà.

Printed in the United States.

Published by
Bordighera, Inc.
John D. Calandra Italian American Institute
25 West 43rd Street, 17th Floor
New York, NY 10036

VIA Folios 84
ISBN 1-59954-047-9
ISBN 978-1-59954-047-4

This book is dedicated to past, present, and future mystics.

CONTENTS

MYSTICS IN THE FAMILY

What does it mean to have mystics in the family?

Great Great Grandfather Giuseppe
fervent and ecstatic in his prayers
was granted the vision of The Souls of Purgatory
marching in procession
singing and holding up one index finger of fire

Great Grandfather Rosario
hypnotized animals to do his bidding
he used his "calamita" magnetism
to discern their thoughts and
read their hearts

Great Grandmother Mattia
told of a small white dog that led her home
when she was a child and lost
the dog disappeared at her door
she knew the little white dog was the soul
of Antonio her late father

Grandfather Francesco
lived in a house full of people and spirits
he saw ghostly goats, cats, dogs, chickens, and persons
walk up and down the stairs
mingling with his living family and friends

My Mother Francesca
always said her late father Pietro
dressed in his work clothes
appeared to her regularly
to warn of trouble ahead

My Father Rosario
always said he was saved in France
during World War Two
by The Madonna of the Rosary
for whom he was named
she commanded him to leave his foxhole
he obeyed and in an instant
a shell destroyed everything on the spot
where he'd just been

What does it mean to have mystics in one's family?
It means that I can claim it came naturally to me
when I stood transported one day
on bustling Ninth Street
all the vendors, hawkers, shoppers, delivery trucks
bathed in an unearthly beautiful light

It means I can say I have the knack
for seeing figures at the foot of my bed
for hearing the knocking of spirits
for witnessing the pranks of ghosts

It means it is a family trait that lets me
hear Mozart's music come out of air conditioners
see black shadowy hats on the heads of those
      soon to depart this world
smell fragrances of roses and aftershave
      when the deceased visit

What does it mean to have mystics in one's family?

It means that one learns
      that life is open
      that life is more.

APPARITION

As a child I was afraid the Blessed Mother
    Our Lady Dressed in Blue
might appear to me, her namesake.
she would come with a terrible message
    I would have to tell the world
    live in a convent with nuns
    meaner than the ones
    who were my teachers
    I'd scrub endless marble floors
    like poor Bernadette of Lourdes

No more macaroni, no more soda
just holy water to drink and one communion wafer a day

The Blessed Mother dictated letters
    to Lucia of Fatima
the first two were about world wars
the third so horrifying
the Pope fainted when he read the words
    told Lucia she had to stay locked up
    never to repeat the message to anyone

I prayed to the Madonna
begging her not to appear to me
    even though I was named for her
    I wasn't holy enough
    I hoped she did not like me
    because I chewed gum, whistled,
    said curse words, punched my brothers

Now in mid-life
I would welcome an apparition
I pray each day to

the uncompromising Mother
the powerful and just Black Madonna of Tindari

She may appear to me anytime
I am not scared   I am ready
she can tell me disasters
    I will listen
no matter the toughness of her demands
I'd tell the world the terrible and the true

in admiration of her goddess strength

I have swords in my own heart now
She can come.

THE BLACK MADONNA OF TINDARI

The Black Madonna of Tindari in Sicily took gentle
vengeance on a woman who came on a pilgrimage, her
baby in her arms.

On climbing the shrine's wind swept cliff, the woman
      exclaimed
"I traveled so far to see somebody blacker than me!"

In an instant, her child disappeared

transported to a spot of dry sand below

in the midst of the Mediterranean Sea

the woman screamed, a boat was sent to rescue her child

she realized that

The Black Madonna of Tindari taught
that racism is a sin.

I AM NOT WHITE

The dentist says my teeth tell of invasions
    mixed blood
the tale of a proud, mongrel people
    I am Sicilian
    I am not white
I will not check the box for white
    on any form

In Sicily
my ancestors recognized white
to be the color of sparkling linens
    towels, tablecloths, sheets
    the color of clouds, seafoam, and bones
not family faces with their
    African, Greek, Arabic, Norman casts

North Italians call us Africans
a Milanese told me that in Sicily
    he heard Africa's drums
I hear them, too,
    especially when
    from across the little stretch of gleaming sea
    North African winds
    blow through our homes

Sicilians left for other lands
trying to escape poverty   injustice
    they prayed to their
    Black Madonna of Tindari
    miraculous advocate for the poor
    for guidance
    packing her image with their clothes

In America at first
they called us colored
Sicilians lynched in the South
    along with Africans
    in the fields, the railroads, the mines

    the children and grandchildren of slaves
    worked at our sides
    taught us American life
    were thought good people, even friends

In America over the years
Sicilians stayed quiet   spoke English
    learned to stand apart
    from those darker sisters and brothers
Sicilians passed to that lighter
    opportunity side of the color line

In America now
some of the Black Madonna's children
    have forgotten her
    ignorant of their roots
    they check the box for white on every form
    no longer aware
    that they are of mixed blood
    the mongrel heirs
    to a proud people of every feature

I cannot forget
when even my teeth tell our story

I will not forget
I have prayed at the Black Madonna's
    ancient, wind-swept shrine at Tindari
I am Sicilian
I am not white.

THE FEAST OF SAINT RITA
May 22, 2007

In our time of war, sadness, and fear
when sickness of bodies, hearts, and minds
troubles the earth
on a day of
cool breezes   green trees
gleaming sun   blue sky
I buy three red roses
ask Saint Rita for peace and healing
for myself   for others
I ask that I be granted enough courage
to comfort and understand
I ask that hearts be calmed   people reconciled

Fourteen years ago
while May sunshine and starshine
streamed through his hospital window
my father lay dying   heavily medicated
he suffered from violent nightmares
he prayed to Saint Rita
as her feast day approached
asking for day time and night time peace of mind
my brother brought him one Saint Rita rose
on her May 22 feast from her church
the next day   peaceful and calm
our father passed from this earthly life
Rita's rose by his bed

One hundred years ago
in a newly built church
at Broad and Federal Street   South Philadelphia
Augustinian friars ministered
to the throngs of Southern Italian and Sicilian immigrants

whose processions, ancient feasts, emotional style
        of prayer
disturbed church hierarchy
troubled American catholics
the friars named the church for Rita Lotti Mancini
fifteenth century wife, mother, Augustinian nun
from the Umbrian town of Cascia

Today with roses in profusion
festooning every altar and pillar
I watch the statue of Rita Lotti Mancini
carried in procession by
men and women of
European, African, Asian, and Mexican descent
down the center aisle of the church named for her
Saint Rita of Cascia

Rita, midwife, herbalist, healer, who cured and comforted
Rita, loyal wife, who loved and helped her husband
Rita, brave, grieving widow, who forgave her husband's
        killers
Rita, loving mother, who steered her sons away from
        vengeance
    and mourned their deaths from sickness she could
        not cure
Rita, reviled as mad for wanting change
    revered for winning the peace for Cascia's warring
        families
Rita, a nun for forty years, who healed the sick, received
        the stigmata,
    asked for roses and figs which grew for her in winter
Rita, a woman who believed nothing is impossible

We, in the pews   holding our roses
with our African, Asian, European, Mexican faces

look up as Rita's stature is placed on the altar
we sing with our Mexican, Asian, African, European voices
the hymn to Saint Rita
a song to Rita of long ago and of today

The Rita who still heals
  who still comforts
The Saint Rita who can whisper
   down through centuries
   in every human language
   a message of peace

Rita is the best of us within us
because Saint Rita channels the force of the universe
which binds us all in love.

SAN GENNARO

I know
San Gennaro is all for Naples and Neapolitans

Although I am Sicilian
I love San Gennaro
    with his vial of blood in the Cathedral of Naples
    with his blood liquefying to keep Naples safe
    with his guarding Vesuvius promising
    to give a warning when it's about to blow

Twenty years ago   in September
I went to the San Gennaro Festival in New York
    bought a little button
    with an image of San Gennaro on it
I wore it pinned to my jacket for three days

On the third day
a friend stopped me in a Philadelphia bookstore
"Why are you wearing a pin of the Pope?"
"He's not the Pope. He's San Gennaro, Patron Saint of
Naples."
"Aren't you Sicilian?"
"Yes, but I love San Gennaro. I love Naples."

The next day
the San Gennaro button disappeared
somehow   someway
his button came off my jacket and
was not found until three years later
when I saw my cat
playing with it in the cellar

I pinned the button on

"San Gennaro, you've returned!"
within the day it disappeared again
never to be found since

I know
San Gennaro is all for Naples and Neapolitans
I still love him   and   Naples, too.

THE INFANT OF PRAGUE WITH A BLACK EYE

The Infant of Prague statue
dressed in the usual hand-sewn ruffled lace dress
    and red satin cape
stands facing outward
in a picture window on Tenth Street

Holding the globe in his left hand
raising his right hand to bless
this Infant of Prague sports a shiner
a nasty black bruise rings his left eye

This Infant of Prague refuses to say how
he once walked into a door   fell off the windowsill
had a mishap with a broom

This Infant of Prague is too proud   too princely
to reveal how he was in a bad street fight
    in his fancy dress
duking it out with a bully

This Infant of Prague won't tell us that
    his pretty boy outfit was a good gimmick
    in the prize fight
where he took a right jab to his left eye
before knocking out his bigger opponent
    in the second round

This Infant of Prague with a black eye
blesses the tusslers   the bookies
the accident prone   the misfortunate
who pass him as he stands there
in the picture window on Tenth Street.

SANT'ANTONIO
For all Anthonys and everybody else

Sant'Antonio   Sant'Antonio   Sant'Antonio Mio
Great Saint Anthony   Great Saint Anthony
I've been praying   praying   praying
to you   you   you   for years
to find me   find me   find me
keys, documents, lovers, books
Saint Anthony, Saint Anthony,
Come around
Something's lost and can't be found
all the lost   all the lost   all the lost you've found
Sant'Antonio Mio
if it's right if it's to be
you've found the lost, lost, lost
and always got me what I needed
Sant'Antonio Mio
St. Anthony   St. Anthony   St. Anthony
come around
St. Anthony called from this way and that way
you covering the earthly continents
and all the galaxies and beyond
finding   finding   finding   the lost, lost, lost
finding even what was not lost
but not yet found
St. Anthony, St. Anthony,
come around
will you   will you   will you
find me a job, job, job?
Dear St. Anthony, Anthony, Anthony
Sant'Antonio Mio
jobs, jobs, jobs   I've had and lost many
jobs, jobs, jobs   I've found and lost a lot
jobs, jobs, jobs   I need a new job   a good job

a job, job, job
Sant'Antonio Mio

Great Kind Dear St. Anthony Anthony Anthony
in all the holy pictures   on all the holy medals
in all the holy churches
you are so popular with the populace
Antonio, Antonio, Antonio
Antonio, Anthony, Antony
your name was ancient
even when you roamed the earth
in a physical body
Antonio, Antonio, Portuguese Preacher
shipwrecked in Sicily   settled in Padua
Antonio   Antonio   Antonio
with your tonsure and Franciscan robe
Saint Anthony of Padua
Antonio   Antonio   Sant'Antonio Mio
with your golden tongue and bread for the poor
holding the Baby Jesus
just as Hermes held Baby Apollo
Antonius   Antonius   Antonius
Antony, Anthony, Antonio
Tonio, Ant, Tony, Nino
Nino, Nini, Nino, Ninuzzu, Nino, Ninitu, Nino
Tony, Tone, Tony
'Ntoni, 'Ntoni, 'Ntoni
Yo, Ant!   Yo, Ant!   Yo, Ant!
Can you find me a miracle job?
Our own only own Anthony   Our St. Anthony
        My St. Anthony

Antony, Antoninus, Antinuous, Antonio
all the ancients converge on your name
all those who carry your finding found name

are now and ever converging
Tonio, Ant, Tony, Nino, Tonino
Tony the Tiger, Tony Martin, Tony Taylor, Tony Bennett
Tony fathers, Tony brothers, Tony godfathers, Tony sons
and everybody's Uncle Tony
Yo, Ant!   Yo, Ant!   Yo, Ant!
An Toe Knee Oh   Toe Knee   An Toe Knee Oh
Toe Knee   Toe Knee   Tony, Tony   Toe Knee
St. Anthony   St. Anthony   St. Anthony
your namesakes
are driving buses, publishing books, cutting pecorino
writing mysteries, making gnocchi, film scores, and
paintings
Tony with the stethoscope
Tony in the laboratory
Nino, Tony, Anthony, Tonino, Tonio, Tone
pointing to the blackboard
sculpting the clay
genuflecting at the altar
Tony at the keyboard
Tony in the courtroom
Tony with the pen   Tony with the drill
Museum Anthony   TV, Radio, Film Anthony
Anthony Head   Anthony Feet   Anthony Hand
Skinny Tony, Fat Tony, Little Anthony, Big Anthony
Anthony with the Imperials, with the guitars, with
        the drums
Anthony with Pets, Pizza, and Pomegranates
Anthony with children and the old
Anthony with wives, boyfriends, girlfriends, lovers
Anthony with the stars, sun, and moon
Anthony Rainbow   Anthony Breeze
partner, brother, nephew, cousin, in-law
barber, baker, scientist, crooner, whistler, gardener
Tony with the vow of silence

Tony with the bullhorn
An Toe Knee Oh   An Toe Knee Oh
Tony, Nino, Tone: musician, poet, conductor, journalist
composer, novelist, gangster, barista   Tony, Nino, Tone

An Toe Knee Oh   An Toe Knee Oh
St. Anthony, St. Anthony,
come around
you, Sweet Antonuccio, you
An Toe Knee Oh
An Toe Knee Oh
Please find me that job and all the lost, lost, lost
all the lost music, toys, people
all the lost jobs, money, time
Tony Oh   Tony Oh   Tony Oh
An   Thon   Eee
An   Thon   Eee
Saint An   Thon   Eee
Oh, Anth   Yo, Anth   Oh, Anth
please, please, please
find me   find me   find me
find me that job, job, job
Oh, a job, Oh, a job, Oh Toe Knee
you can do it
An   Toe   Knee   Oh
An   Toe   Knee   Oh
you can find me a job, a job, Oh, Toe Knee

Sweet Tone   Sweet Tone   Sweet Tone Knee Oh
a job, please   a job, please   a job, please
Toe Knee Oh   Toe Knee Oh   Toe Knee Oh
Sant'Antonio
Sant'Antonio
Sant'Antonio Mio.

EYE OPERATION

The green cloaked men are wheeling me past the
            yellow walls

They've pasteled me with five rear injections and
            arm pin-holes

As they park by swinging doors I wait my turn
to be sliced at throbbing optic nerve,
like Saint Lucy, I'll have eye pieces
miraculous, gleaming and forlorn upon a plate

Blue bottles line the wall
alive in three dimensional grace
all smile like sky-gods above the sacrificial mount
the rolling bed glides to an altared room of pinkish blue
where masked priests shall flay away the layers to
that naked nerve that catches prism light
here they'll pierce the tiny arbiter of my world view
which hammers along with the heart of mind

I stare at white headlight eye above a strapped bed
and hold a fisted arm toward a steel needle voice
oozing in pneumatic count, one, two, three
            "God, I offer thee…"

The headlight eye blinks
and the shades of the underworld begin

MY MOTHER'S PRAYER LIST

They asked her
Pray for me
Pray for us
Pray for me
    and she did

My mother kept a list
a long list   a long handwritten list
she kept a long handwritten list
of all those who asked her to pray

She kept a long list
a long handwritten list
until the day she died
when I found the list
the long handwritten list
in her housedress pocket

My mother wrote the names
clear on the page   she wrote the names
in her neat Palmer Method script
she wrote each name followed by a dash
she wrote name, dash, request
of all those who asked her to pray

They asked her
Pray for me
Pray for us
Pray for me
    and she did

She prayed for health, for family, for friends
      for peace in the home

and peace in the world

She prayed for good marriages, for troubled children
for surgery survival, for house sales, and school
exams

She prayed for courage, for serenity, for patience
for driving tests, blood tests
and for finding a job

They asked her
Pray for me
Pray for us
Pray for me
    and she did

My mother cooked, cleaned, went to church, washed
clothes, shopped,
said the rosary, tended the garden
always with the list
the long list   the long handwritten list
in her pocket
to help her remember

They asked her
Pray for me
Pray for us
Pray for me
    and she did

in her home   in her gentle way
my mother loved her husband, honored her parents
raised four children
minded grandchildren

always with the list   the long list
the long handwritten list in her pocket

They asked her
Pray for me
Pray for us
Pray for me
      and she did

My mother cooked meals for shut-ins
nursed the sick
mourned the dead
gave comfort   offered courage
always with the list   the long list
the long handwritten list in her pocket

My mother laughed, ate, celebrated
made fabulous cakes and sumptuous dinners

She fed the birds, cared for the cat
swept the sidewalk, watched the stories on TV
she sang, wrote letters, chatted, listened to music
always with the list   the long list
the long handwritten list   in her pocket

Her life was a prayer

They asked her
Pray for me
Pray for us
Pray for me
      and she did

She honored all the requests for prayers
until the day she died

when I found the list   the long list
my mother's long handwritten list
in her housedress pocket
her long handwritten list of all those
who asked my graceful mother to pray

Her life was a prayer

They asked her
Pray for me
Pray for us
Pray for me
    and she did.

CHICKPEAS

This is how we pass down our history
hold up a handful of chickpeas
say "ciceri" in Sicilian tongue

This is how we pass down our history
through the ages
whether we could read or write or not
in countryside   mountainside   seaside

This is how we pass down our history
my father holds up a handful of roasted chickpeas
makes us repeat the word after him
"ciceri" "ciceri" "ciceri"
we are children anxious to leave the table
play   laugh   shout   in English
in Philadelphia   USA
where our family set down roots
fragile and tough as chickpea plants

we were Mediterranean for millenia
        American for two decades

This is how we pass down our history
my father holds up a handful of roasted chickpeas
this night they are snacks with wine
my grandfather tells us we should always have
a handful of chickpeas in our pocket as he does
in case we get hungry
in case we are served food we cannot eat
the chickpeas will sustain us
"ciceri" "ciceri" "ciceri"
say "ciceri" "ciceri" "ciceri"

My father holds up a handful of chickpeas
this humble   exalted   Mediterranean food
in a Philadelphia kitchen
we must learn to say
"ciceri" "ciceri" "ciceri"

This is how we pass down our history
over the centuries across oceans
countryside   mountainside   seaside

My father tells us the history of the proud and oppressed
in 1282 the Sicilians rose up
against the arrogant haughty French
who taxed and insulted the Sicilian people
took liberties with Sicilian women
lounged in Sicilian houses

Sicilians were patient   waiting for their chance
to overthrow the French
the chance came on Easter Monday in Palermo
in front of the Church of the Holy Spirit
the armed French soldiers stood guard
over the Palermitans thronging the piazza
as they headed to the Church's Vespers service
the French soldier Drouette, filled with Sicilian wine,
stopped a beautiful young woman
walking to church with her husband
Drouette grabbed her as if to search for weapons
fondled her breasts
her husband shouted, "Death to the French!"
the crowd surged   the fighting began
Drouette fell   stabbed in the heart

Messengers carried the signal throughout the island
the time had come   "Death to the French!"

Sicilians rose up
with knives, rocks, sticks, stones, canes, swords
west to east   east to west
north to south   south to north
"Death to the French!"
thousands of French hunted down and killed
as the signal traveled the island's
countryside   mountainside   seaside

My father tells us some French tried to escape
dressed in peasant clothes
they hid in countryside   mountainside   seaside
they were caught and killed my father says
my grandfather holds up a handful of chickpeas
says "ciceri" "ciceri" "ciceri"
my father says the French could not pronounce the
        word correctly
"ciceri" "ciceri" "ciceri"
humble   exalted   powerful   chickpeas

"ciceri" "ciceri" "ciceri"

If you were Sicilian you said "ciceri"
if you were Sicilian
Go in Peace   The Madonna Bless You
in your countryside   mountainside   seaside   home
you lived on to bless
the exalted   humble   powerful
"ciceri" "ciceri" "ciceri"

This is how we pass down our history
my father and grandfather holding chickpeas in their
        palms
telling us how Sicilians chopped up French dead
shipped them back to France pickled in barrels

our skin goosebumps as we listen
our eyes widen with horror and wonder

think how it would be if Sicilians held up chickpeas
they would kill you if you did not say it right
"ciceri" "ciceri" "ciceri"
you feel sorry for those French
sent to a faraway land where they were hated
where they could not pronounce
"ciceri" "ciceri" "ciceri"

you feel relief as you say
"ciceri" "ciceri" "ciceri"
you would live and be sustained by
humble   exalted   powerful   chickpeas

you are proud
as you take a handful of roasted chickpeas
eat them slowly
your father and grandfather smile
when you say "ciceri" "ciceri" "ciceri"
because even though you live in Philadelphia USA
your family was saved nearly eight hundred years ago
in countryside   mountainside   seaside
when they said "ciceri" "ciceri" "ciceri"
therefore, this is how we must pass down our history
hold up a handful of chickpeas
say "ciceri" in Sicilian tongue.

THE ELIXIR OF PIETRA RIMITA

Way up in the Sicilian mountains
    higher up than nearby
    San Pier Niceto, my family's village,
there is a dusty trail
leading to Pietra Rimita
    the giant hermit stone
    where there is a glacial spring
    with a water tap
    dug into the mountain face
    where cold, cold water flows
    delicious water
    delectable water
    pure   full-bodied   mineral-filled
    cold, clear water
    revered by the locals
    for its restorative powers

Up there on the mountain trail
with goats, sheep, herders walking past
up there on the mountain trail
in cars, trucks, motorcycles, and on foot
scores of people come everyday
to fill their bottles and jugs
with cold, clean mountain water

On my first summertime visit to Sicily
the heat and high altitude
had stricken me with constant thirst
to everyone's alarm
I drank glass after glass of limonata
              aranciata
              caffè freddo
              even Coca Cola

but what I desired most and drank most was water
right from Zia Antonia's kitchen sink

One hot, sunny day, Zia Antonia hitched a ride
with neighbors going up to Pietra Rimita
to fill their big ten liter jugs with
the special spring water
Zia Antonia and I sat in the backseat
with our empty plastic jugs in our laps

as the neighbor drove
the ear-popping, hairpin turns

There at the mountain tap we waited in line
the neighbors filled their jugs
I helped Zia Antonia fill our jugs
with cold, lovely water

I cupped my hands   took a sip
    the water was wonderful
    beyond what I had ever tasted
I wanted more but behind us
was a man whose beat-up, open-backed truck
held a hundred empty glass bottles
Zia said he'd taken orders
would deliver the beautiful water for a fee

When we got back to San Pier Niceto
Zia Antonia opened one jug
poured some of the Pietra Rimita water
into a large glass pitcher
she placed the pitcher on the kitchen table
covering it with a white dish towel
she put the jug in the refrigerator
and stored the other jugs in the back room

Zia allowed me a small glass of the spring water
I gulped it down so fast
my Aunt said she feared for my health
I was not to drink too much of
the delicious, delectable mountain water
she said the water had restorative powers
but it also had the ability
to make a person "dimagrire"
lose weight   become too thin
the water was to be sipped, savored
not guzzled

This spring water was an elixir

At meals, I was watched when
I drank my little glass of Pietra Rimita elixir
I was scolded for pouring myself another glass
I was reprimanded for drinking too fast
Zia Antonia worried I'd lose weight
become thin and weak
I said I could stand to lose a few pounds
I said if I brought this water to America
where everyone wanted to lose weight
we could make a fortune

Zia Antonia scoffed
she said this water was powerful
and no joking matter

One night after my Aunt had gone to bed
my throat was parched
I craved that spring water
I craved the Pietra Rimita elixir
I tip-toed downstairs from my second floor bedroom
into the kitchen

as quietly as I could I opened the fridge
Zia Antonia called from her upstairs bedroom
"Don't drink that water!"
"I'm not drinking it!" I called back
I tip-toed slowly to the kitchen table
slowly, carefully
lifted the dish towel from the pitcher
"I can hear you with the towel" cried Zia Antonia
"Come upstairs! Go to sleep! You've had enough water!"

I took a tiny sip of Pietra Rimita water
    right from the pitcher
    made my way back upstairs

The next day at our noon-time meal
I was lectured again by my aunt and other relatives
on the dangers of that
delicious, delectable water
as I sipped the powerful water from a little glass
I was instructed that if I wanted
even a tiny bit more of the spring water
I had to mix it with wine

Zia Antonia did not want me
to return to the States
skinny, skinny   fragile, fragile
    weak, weak

my parents would think she did not feed me
there I would be in the USA
so weak
so fragile
a thin, thin young woman
so frail she couldn't even stand up
all because I drank too much

delectable, delicious, wonderful
Pietra Rimita water.

MASS AT LA MATRICE
The Mother Church

Zia Antonia was proud
to show me off at
the eleven o'clock mass
at the mother church of San Pier Niceto

I walked on her arm
she a half century older
in her kerchief and Sunday flowered dress
I wore the chapel veil she gave me
and an embroidered dress from France

on the way to church
we passed men lounging at the bar
and caught up to the women
who told me my grandmother
taught them the times tables
      how were my parents in America?
      did I like the village?
      wasn't my aunt strong and vigorous for her age?

inside the church
      marble, mosaics, tiles, and stuccoed walls
      so much cooler than the street
we lit candles to the Madonna
I followed my aunt to her usual seat

I didn't know the words
      to the songs she sang

I prayed in English in my head.

ROSE PETALS

The lady around the corner
whose yard is across from mine
wants me to chop down my rose tree
because she says all her sweeping
of rose petals
in the summer heat
is killing her

Warm winds lift deep red petals into the air
they land in my yard, her yard, the alley
I think they make a luxurious carpet

I tell the lady around the corner
whose yard is across from mine
that when the time is right
I will trim the branches
she is not satisfied
"Chop it down!
Cut it to the ground!"
I tell her not to get nervous
she screams louder
"All those rose petals! All this sweeping!
I can't take it!
Twenty, thirty times a day
I'm out there in the heat
sweeping and sweeping and sweeping
I'll soon be dead from a heart attack!
You and your rose tree will have killed me!"

Three years ago
the lady around the corner
whose yard is across from mine
told our neighbor Angelina

to chop down her peach tree
she said we were all going to die
from the germs brought by all the rats
coming to eat peaches
from Angelina's tree

The peach tree had an intoxicating fragrance
Angelina gave dozens of delicious peaches
to all the neighbors each summer

yet the lady around the corner
whose yard is across from mine
cried and screamed
she said she was calling
The Board of Health

Although nobody had actually seen any rats
Angelina made her son chop down
the beautiful peach tree

Lady around the corner,
whose yard is across from mine,
I hope you don't die
a death from rose petals
with a broom in your hand
on a hot July day

Lady around the corner,
whose yard is across from mine,
I wish you could learn to love
the softness and scent of rose petals
the fragrance and flavor of peaches

I wish you could learn to love
the bounty of nature
which sweetens our city living.

TRASHING PEOPLE OVER PIE
For Barbara

Sitting with plates of vegan pie on our knees
we   at the party
lovers of animals   ethereal sensualists

we begin to trash
    the rich poet who hates all poems but his own
    the dentist who stole another's lover
    the editor who writes six-page hate letters
    to imaginary enemies

we trash people over pie
    high schoolers who call us names
    neighbors who refuse to say hello
    homeowners who burn down houses
    of those who are different

we trash them all over apricot pie
loading on dollops of rice dream

we trash
    right wing Iowans
    drunk driving Levittowners
    survivalist Jerseyites
    scary bicycle thieves who say
    they are from South P.

we   at the party
with our full plates and our woes

are we any closer to the angels
because we eat vegan pie

we   do   because   we   can

trash people over pie.

WINDOW ROCK

In Navajoland
I stand in awe of startling red rock
the burning blue sky
the ancient smell of sage

I sit in a hogan with my ulcer flaring
the medicine man is ready for the healing ceremony
he has asked me to bring two items
that tell from where I've come
I place before him a piece of black lava
    from towering fuming Etna
    volcano of Sicily
    my ancestral home much loved and visited
    where dear ones are buried
    where dear ones still reside
I place before him a tiny Liberty Bell
    from Philadelphia
    the city where my family came years ago
    in search of freedom from hunger, from disaster,
        from injustice

I bow my head before the medicine man's blessings
I bow before his songs   his sand paintings
he says I am healed

That night under countless stars and gleaming moon
I cannot open my plastic bottle of ulcer medicine
neither can my Navajo friends
they tell me it is alright   no need to worry
mysterious things must happen here they say
if you wish to learn to walk the rainbow path
    where beauty is before you and
    beauty is behind you

no need for ulcer medicine
when different medicine works inside

My pain subsides
I eat blue corn   chili peppers   frybread
drink black coffee
all through Arizona   New Mexico   Utah
with my friends
they remind me
I will stay healed

I will stay blessed
as long as I remember that
all is sacred   all is beauty
before and behind me

as I try to walk the rainbow path.

CANYON DE CHELLY

A woman prays at Canyon De Chelly
the sun rises over
Spider Grandmother's sandstone spire

      distant starshine
      warm first light
      sacred rocks, juniper trees, sage brush
      the wind is a presence
      one eagle flies overhead

spirit guides, come
animal mentors, come
a woman prays at Canyon De Chelly

      seashells of past ocean
      dry sands of the wash
      change and stay
      ancient Anasazi cliff dwellings
      present Navajo hogans
      change and stay

      hawk and owl
      sheep and herders
      cornfield and stream
      trees and scrub
      prairie dog and mouse
      change and stay
      sing the power of the pulse
      the holiness of sunshine on stone

a woman prays at Canyon De Chelly
changes   changes
and stays.

NONNA'S CUP
For my niece, Mary

A young Sicilian woman   new to Philadelphia
shopping at the Ninth Street outdoor market
was drawn to an ornate cup
on the Syrian vendor's cart
she loved all the beautiful china, glassware,
and linens he sold

Her basket filled with swiss chard, potatoes, apples
the night's meal
Mattia still had a few coins to spend
she bought the cup
with its red roses and gilded green leaves
everything carved in relief
with the words   below the rim
in embossed gold letters
THINK OF ME

My Nonna Mattia did not know
the words' meaning
she could not read nor write in any language
she could not ask the vendor
they only spoke in gestures and nods

At home, she placed her prized cup
on a shelf behind the cupboard's glass door
she savored the cup's beauty everyday
nobody was allowed to drink from it

When Mattia's children
learned to read
they told Mattia what the cup's words meant
THINK OF ME

my great grandmother loved her cup even more

When Nonno Pietro died
Nonna Mattia went to live
in the home of her youngest girl
taking only a few possessions
she gave her precious cup to my mother
her granddaughter
who had always admired with Nonna
the cup with its golden words
THINK OF ME
My mother put the cup in her china closet
with all her own best dishes and cups
when Nonna visited
she viewed her cup through the glass
in its prominent place
THINK OF ME

When Nonna died
my mother took out the cup
held it up   told me
"Let's always think of Nonna
when we look at this cup"
THINK OF ME

Through the years we always thought of Nonna
and we always made sure her special cup was safe
especially when we took out the best dishes and cups
for holiday meals

When my mother died
I took the treasured cup to my home
placed it behind the glass of my kitchen cabinet
where I can see it every day
THINK OF ME

I think of Nonna Mattia
love her   thank her
I think of my Mother
love her   thank her
THINK OF ME
my great grandmother   my mother
someday me
when I'm gone and
my niece places the ornate china cup
somewhere in her home
THINK OF ME
think of us.

NUMBER 12
For Francesca Guaetta Famà

October with its flaming leaves
bright sky and crisp air
was my mother's favorite month
October 2 was her birthday
while October 4, the feast of her patron
Saint Francis of Assisi, was her name day
on the first Sunday of every October
the month to honor Italians
the Procession of Saints from St. Nicholas of Tolentine
      Church
passed by her front door on its way
back to the parish's Italian Festival

My mother's spirit was strong beside me
on an October day
when I walked a bit with the Procession of Saints
then wandered the booths and stalls of
the Italian Festival with its
food, music, rides, entertainment, and
games of chance

My mother was famous for
winning prizes at street festivals and
on the boardwalk down the shore
she'd put down a dime, a quarter, a dollar
win for her children, her grandchildren, herself
stuffed animals, dolls, toys, plants, flowers,
whiskey, wine, pastries

I hesitated in front of a dollar a spin booth
Should I play?   Will I waste my money?
Is 3, 7, or 17 the best number to play?

My mother's spirit was strong beside me
I heard her voice whisper into my ear
"Put the dollar on Number 12"
I pulled out a dollar, placed it on the number 12 square
the lady at the booth told me to spin
The Wheel of Fortune
I spun the wheel
astounded when it stopped at 12

My mother's spirit was strong beside me
exultant
as I won a huge colander of Italian groceries
sustenance   fortune
the kitchen   the home
a colander of groceries
with magical number 12
in the clear air of her favorite month
my mother's spirit was strong beside me.

TIP THE HAT YOU GOT

Saluta cu cappeddu chi hai
my grandfather, Pietro Guaetta, used to say

I called him Grandpop
my loving, patient, Sicilian grandfather
always answered all my questions

Grandpop, I asked
What does saluta cu cappeddu chi hai
mean?

He said
Saluta cu cappeddu chi hai
Tip the hat you got

Grandpop, what does that mean?

He said
if you got on a little cap
    you tip your little cap
if you got on a great, big, Texas ten gallon hat
    you tip your great, big, Texas ten gallon hat
if you got on a top hat, straw hat, or derby
    you tip your top hat, straw hat, or derby

Grandpop, what does that mean?

He said
Saluta cu cappeddu chi hai
Tip the hat you got
if you are poor
if you are rich
it does not matter

Respect yourself
Respect others

Do your best with what you got

Saluta cu cappeddu chi hai
Tip the hat you got.

FAILING TIME AND MONEY
For Gabriella

When I tutored you, Gabriella,
I had the little clock faces ready and
pennies, nickels, dimes, quarters for
our review of first grade lessons

When you saw the clocks you told me
"I failed time"
Eyeing the stacks of coins you told me
"I failed money, too"

I did not tell you then
that I've also failed time
with my watch strapped to my wrist
I cannot squeeze into the passing hours
all that I want to do

I've failed money, too,
always broke   my hard earned money
never enough as
I wonder how to pay my bills

Yet, I think, dear child,
that time failed us
    when people long ago made up
    such things as seconds, minutes, hours
    days, weeks, months, years, centuries
    millennia

If we divide the vastness of eternity
    in a different way
You, sweet child of seven,
might be a few minutes old

I might be nine instead of fifty-nine

The more we count
the more time fails us

Money, oh money, Gabriella,
these raggedy greenbacks
these tiny dimes   heavy nickels
plain old pennies   evolving quarters
are even phonier than time
time at least has the pacing of the sun and moon
money has only those in charge
to tell us to agree that money is worth
     what they tell us
     so we can trade it in for
     what we need and what we don't need

Money must fail us all
there is always a price tag
we cannot afford

Since time is money in our society
I must teach you, dear child,
these clock faces and these coins

I must also tell you, Gabriella,
we are both rich in spirit and nature
we have eternity on our side

Let us both fail money and time.

OREGANO

In September
Angela and Giovannino
pick oregano they've grown
in their Sicilian field

In October
they tie bunches of dried oregano
with pretty colored ribbons
give them to Ann and Steve
visiting American cousins
to take back to the U.S. relatives
with best wishes

Ann and Steve
carry fragrant oregano
from San Pier Niceto
in large plastic bags
squeezed into carry-on luggage
they fly from Palermo to Boston
where the customs inspector asks
What is this?
Oregano Ann answers
What is it?
an herb   a spice
What is it used for?
for salads, for sauces, for meat, fish, pizza
Pizza! he cries
How much pizza you gonna make
with all this?
Ann laughs
the inspector lets her keep the oregano

Ann and Steve
visit Rob and Mindy in Boston
hand them some oregano
board a flight from Boston
home to San Diego
where they portion out bunches
send handpicked
sun dried   aromatic   oregano
by priority U.S. Mail
to relatives in New York, Ohio,
Nevada and Pennsylvania

Sicilian oregano now sits
in my Philadelphia kitchen
with its scent of sun, sea, mountain field
with its touch of
Angela, Giovannino, Ann, Steve
the loving family hands
that link us
across oceans and continents
to ancient Sicily
our first home.

REFLECTION

As I open my laptop
I catch my reflection on the blank screen
My grandmother, Domenica, stares back at me
with that wary, haughty tilt of the chin

here I am at six in the morning
on the sofa   in a nightshirt
with the same expression
Grandmom wore when she posed for
formal photographs or debated politics

There for a moment
I see that burning intensity around the eyes
that Grandmom had when she labored
over her sewing machine
turning out dresses and pants
I wonder if this is how I look
bending over a keyboard
to turn out poems

In the screen's reflection
Hints of my grandmother's wedding portrait
        my high school graduation picture
        that expression of wonder
        at the telling of tender or tragic tales
those looks borne in our genes
all through the fields, factories
                kitchens, classrooms
                bedrooms and parlors

all flash in the quick minute
before I press the computer's power button
and brightness overtakes me.

OLD LADIES

I tell my sister-in-law
my young neighbor, Josh, power-washes
his sidewalk, front steps, windows, and house front
every week

She says
"The old ladies must love him!"
I think but do not say
all the old ladies on this street are gone

Margherita, Rosie, Annie, Josie, and Marì
Those old ladies who
swept and washed their steps and sidewalks every day
shoveled snow in slippers
with only sweaters tossed over their housedresses
all those hardy old ladies are gone

Margherita, Rosie, Annie, Josie, and Marì
who cooked and cleaned all day
then sat in a circle on beach chairs
outside on summer evenings
drinking coffee, laughing, and talking

Margherita, Rosie, Annie, Josie, and Marì
who when I was a young neighbor
offered me biscotti and kind words
as I trudged home late from work

all those old ladies are gone

Now, I am one of the old ladies of this street
Vicki, Patti, Roe, Annette, and me
        in our sixties

with grinding jobs
we hardly see each other

We sweep the sidewalk on occasion
once in a while throw a bucket of water
onto front steps
we pay others to shovel snow

The young neighbors never knew
Margherita, Rosie, Annie, Josie, and Marì
Those robust old ladies of years past
they only know their replacements
Vicki, Patti, Roe, Annette, and me
the new old ladies on this street
who never sit outside on beach chairs
duties press us
as we rush here and there

The young neighbors smile at us
they show concern
we offer a word and a wave
as we dash away

On this street
the young neighbors clean, laugh, shovel snow
they sit outside on beach chairs on summer evenings
tending babies, dogs, and flowers
as the new old ladies
Vicki, Patti, Roe, Annette, and me
hurry   hurry   hurry   along.

DISH TOWEL SPEAKS

She uses cold water   cold water   cold water
then she dries herself off with me

I am a beautiful terrycloth dish towel
with a blue and white teapot design
Aunt Angie selected me
especially for her as a housewarming gift
told her, "You are really going to enjoy this towel!"

I live with other towels in the closet
I am washed and rested until it is time
For my duty on the hook by the sink
where cold water   cold water   cold water
flows from the tap
she uses cold water   cold water   cold water
then dries herself off with me

She cooks pasta al dente
testing for doneness she burns her lower lip
on a scalding spaghetti strand
she splashes on cold water   cold water   cold water
then she dries herself off with me

She tears off a sheet of plastic wrap
slices her thumb on the serrated side of the box
blood spurts everywhere
she splashes on cold water   cold water   cold water
then she dries herself off with me

She tosses cold water   cold water   cold water
into her itchy allergic nose
then she dries herself off with me
she runs cold water   cold water   cold water

on her wrists to cool down from summer heat
then she dries herself off with me
she dabs cold water   cold water   cold water
on her forehead to calm her headache
then she dries herself off with me
she throws cold water   cold water   cold water
on her swollen eyes as she cries over losses and pain
then she dries herself off with me

I like when she rinses fruit and vegetables
in cold water   cold water   cold water
then she dries herself off with me
tossing me over her shoulder as
she walks from room to room
I am proud when she gazes at my teapot design
Though I worry that my blue edges are fraying

I believe she needs me
I believe Aunt Angie was right
she enjoys me
with all the cooking and crying she does
with all the mishaps with pots, pans,
dishes, cups, and hearts
with all the cold water   cold water   cold water
she runs from the tap
she needs me
she enjoys me

she uses cold water   cold water   cold water
then she dries herself off with me.

THE SCENT OF AFTERSHAVE

A scent of aftershave sometimes fills rooms
sweet   bracing   clean   comforting

It is my father's spirit visiting

My aunt smells aftershave in her kitchen
While peering into a pot of sauce
she turns to see if someone climbed the backstairs
No, she knows it is her brother visiting

My mother awakens to aftershave in her winter bedroom
she questions the sheets, "Is it detergent?"
No, she knows it is her husband visiting

My father was a barber
every morning he splashed aftershave on himself
then onto customers in his shop
he took aftershave from his traveling barber case
when he gave haircuts and shaves
in offices, bedrooms, parlors, kitchens, and cellars

The scent of aftershave fills my parlor
as I drink tea and face a stack of bills
I rush out the front door   no one is passing
no scent of aftershave outside

In the parlor my father's fragrance lingers
he is visiting
"Daddy, Daddy," I whisper, "You are here."

INTERVENTIONS OF MY GRANDMOTHER
Domenica Bongiovanni Guaetta

On a hot August night in 1926
my teenaged grandmother watched
her father rage against her sister's elopement
    in his wrath he grabbed the family photo
    ripped his errant daughter from the page
    threw her image into the cooking fire

My grandmother burned her fingers
snatching her sister's photo from the flames
    she patched her sister's torn face and leg
    with cellophane
    taping the image back into the family photo

My grandmother then waited for the news:
her runaway sister and her new husband
    had been in a car crash
    deep gashes marred her sister's face and leg
    she was injured   not dead

On a sunny September morning in 1944
my grandmother came in from hanging clothes in
      her yard
    when all of a sudden
    the little bronze Statue of Liberty souvenir
    a present from my soldier father
    who was courting her daughter
    fell off a shelf in the living room

My grandmother's thoughts raced to my father
    on the frontlines of World War Two
    she rushed to the Statue of Liberty
    saw a hairline crack along its spine

she filled the crack with paste

My grandmother then waited for the news:
my father had been wounded in battle in France
    pieces of shrapnel pierced his spine
    he was injured   not dead

My grandmother never bragged about her deeds
she told the stories
showed the mended photo and mended souvenir

said she prayed as she intervened

She only took gentle credit for helping Fate.

ABOUT THE AUTHOR

MARIA FAMÀ is the author of five books of poetry. Her work appears in numerous publications and anthologies. In 1998, she was named a finalist in the Allen Ginsberg Poetry Awards. Famà has read her poetry in many cities across the country, read one of her stories on National Public Radio, co-founded a video production company, and was awarded the 2002 and 2005 Aniello Lauri Award for Creative Writing. In 2006, she won the Amy Tritsch Needle Award for Poetry. Her book, *Looking for Cover*, was published in 2008 by Bordighera Press. Maria Famà lives and works in Philadelphia.

Author photograph by Frank Fama, July 4, 2012.

VIA FOLIOS

A refereed book series dedicated to the culture of Italians and Italian Americans.

DANIELA GIOSEFFI, Escaping La Vita Della Cucina, Vol. 83, Italian American Studies, $20
LORENZO DELBOCA, Polentoni, Vol. 82, Italian Studies, $20
SAMUEL GHELLI, A Reference Grammar, Vol. 81, Italian American Studies, $20
ROSS TALARICO, Sled Run, Vol. 80, Fiction, $15
FRED MISURELLA, Only Sons, Vol. 79, Fiction, $17
FRANK LENTRICCHIA, The Portable Lentricchia, Vol. 78, Fiction, $17
RICHARD VETERE, The Other Colors in a Snow Storm, Vol. 77, Poetry, $10
GARIBALDI LAPOLLA, Fire in the Flesh, Vol. 76, Fiction, $25
GEORGE GUIDA, The Pope Stories, Vol. 75, Fiction, $15
ROBERT VISCUSI, Ellis Island, Vol. 74, Poetry, $28
ELENA GIANINI BELOTI, The Bitter Taste of Strangers Bread, Vol. 73, Fiction, $24
PINO APRILE, Terroni, Vol. 72, Italian American Studies, $20
EMANUEL DI PASQUALE, Harvest, Vol. 71, Poetry, $10
ROBERT ZWEIG, Return to Naples, Vol. 70, Memoir, $16
AIROS & CAPPELLI, Guido, Vol. 69, Italian American Studies, $12
FRED GARDAPHÉ, Moustache Pete is Dead! Long Live Moustache Pete!, Vol. 67,
  Literature/Oral History, $12
PAOLO RUFFILLI, Dark Room/Camera oscura, Vol. 66, Poetry, $11
HELEN BAROLINI, Crossing the Alps, Vol. 65, Fiction, $14
COSMO FERRARA, Profiles of Italian Americans, Vol. 64, Italian American, $16
GIL FAGIANI, Chianti in Connecticut, Vol. 63, Poetry, $10
BASSETTI & D'ACQUINO, Italic Lessons, Vol. 62, Italian American Studies, $10
CAVALIERI & PASCARELLI, Eds., The Poet's Cookbook, Vol. 61, Poetry/Recipes, $12
EMANUEL DI PASQUALE, Siciliana, Vol. 60, Poetry, $8
NATALIA COSTA, Ed., Bufalini, Vol. 59, Poetry
RICHARD VETERE, Baroque, Vol. 58, Fiction
LEWIS TURCO, La Famiglia/The Family, Vol. 57, Memoir, $15
NICK JAMES MILETI, The Unscrupulous, Vol. 56, Humanities, $20
BASSETTI, ACCOLLA, D'AQUINO, Italici: An Encounter with Piero Bassetti, Vol. 55, Italian
  Studies, $8
GIOSE RIMANELLI, The Three-legged One, Vol. 54, Fiction, $15
CHARLES KLOPP, Bele Antiche Stòrie, Vol. 53, Criticism, $25
JOSEPH RICAPITO, Second Wave, Vol. 52, Poetry, $12
GARY MORMINO, Italians in Florida, Vol. 51, History, $15
GIANFRANCO ANGELUCCI, Federico F., Vol. 50, Fiction, $15
ANTHONY VALERIO, The Little Sailor, Vol. 49, Memoir, $9
ROSS TALARICO, The Reptilian Interludes, Vol. 48, Poetry, $15
RACHEL GUIDO DE VRIES, Teeny Tiny Tino's Fishing Story, Vol. 47, Children's Lit, $6
EMANUEL DI PASQUALE, Writing Anew, Vol. 46, Poetry, $15
MARIA FAMÀ, Looking For Cover, Vol. 45, Poetry, $12
ANTHONY VALERIO, Toni Cade Bambara's One Sicilian Night, Vol. 44, Poetry, $10
EMANUEL CARNEVALI, Dennis Barone, Ed., Furnished Rooms, Vol. 43, Poetry, $14
BRENT ADKINS, et al., Ed., Shifting Borders, Negotiating Places, Vol. 42, Proceedings, $18
GEORGE GUIDA, Low Italian, Vol. 41, Poetry, $11
GARDAPHÈ, GIORDANO, TAMBURRI, Introducing Italian Americana, Vol. 40, Italian
  American Studies, $10

Published by Bordighera, Inc., an independently owned not-for-profit scholarly
organization that has no legal affiliation with the University of Central Florida and the
John D. Calandra Italian American Institute, Queens College/CUNY.